WHOSE NOSE IS THAT?

By Mary Griffin

Gareth Stevens
PUBLISHING

Please visit our website, www.garethstevens.com. For a free color catalog of all our high-quality books, call toll free 1-800-542-2595 or fax 1-877-542-2596.

Library of Congress Cataloging-in-Publication Data

Names: Griffin, Mary, 1978- author.
Title: Whose nose is that? / Mary Griffin.
Description: New York : Gareth Stevens Publishing, [2024] | Series: Animal
    bodies | Includes index.
Identifiers: LCCN 2022047255 (print) | LCCN 2022047256 (ebook) | ISBN
    9781538286449 (library binding) | ISBN 9781538286432 (paperback) | ISBN
    9781538286456 (ebook)
Subjects: LCSH: Nose–Juvenile literature.
Classification: LCC QL947 .G75 2024 (print) | LCC QL947 (ebook) | DDC
    599.14/4–dc23/eng/20220929
LC record available at https://lccn.loc.gov/2022047255
LC ebook record available at https://lccn.loc.gov/2022047256

Published in 2024 by
Gareth Stevens Publishing
2544 Clinton Street
Buffalo, NY 14224

Copyright © 2024 Gareth Stevens Publishing

Designer: Tanya Dellaccio Keeney
Editor: Therese Shea

Photo credits: Cover, p.1 Tatyana Vyc/Shutterstock.com; pp. 5, 7, 24 (anteater) Azahara Perez/
Shutterstock.com; pp. 9, 11 Zi Magine/Shutterstock.com; pp. 13, 15 Lee Ph/Shutterstock.com;
pp. 17, 19 Dmitry Kalinovsky/Shutterstock.com; pp. 21, 23, 24 (nostril) Thorsten Spoerlein/
Shutterstock.com; p. 24 (underground) omad_Soul/Shutterstock.com.

Printed in the United States of America

CPSIA compliance information: Batch #CSGS24: For further information contact Gareth Stevens, at 1-800-542-2595.

Find us on

Contents

Let's look at animal noses!
Look at this long nose.

It's an anteater.
It smells 40 times better
than a person can!

Look at this pointy nose.

It's a shark.
Water goes in and out
of its nose!

Look at this wet nose.

13

It's a dog.
A wet nose helps it
smell and cool down!

Look at this round nose.

It's a pig.
Pigs can smell things
deep underground!

Look at this black nose.

It's a cheetah.
Its large nostrils help it
take in air and run fast!

Words to Know

anteater

nostril

underground

Index